MW00512046

Mothers
are
Forever

Mary Carlisle Beasley

WG
WALNUT GROVE PRESS
NASHVILLE, TN

Mothers

are
Forever

Mary Carlisle Beasley

Walnut Grove Press
Nashville, TN 37203

2nd Edition
ISBN 1-58334-137-4

The ideas expressed in this book are not, in all cases, exact quotations, as some have been edited for clarity and brevity. In all cases, the author has attempted to maintain the speaker's original intent. In some cases, material for this book was obtained from secondary sources, primarily print media. While every effort was made to ensure the accuracy of these sources, the accuracy cannot be guaranteed. For additions, deletions, corrections or clarifications in future editions of this text, please write Walnut Grove Press.

Printed in the United States of America
Cover & Page Layout Design by Bart Dawson
Cover Photo: www.comstock.com
1 2 3 4 5 6 7 8 9 10 • 02 03 04 05 06 07 08 09 10

Acknowledgments: The author is indebted to Angela Freeman, Dick and Mary Freeman, Ron Smith, Jim Gallery, and to the creative staff at Walnut Grove Press.

For Mom

Table of Contents

Introduction

*M*otherhood, other claims to the contrary, is the world's oldest profession—and its most important one. This little book celebrates the joys and responsibilities of the job.

Lin Yutang observed, "Of all the rights of women, the greatest is to be a mother." Yutang understood that a good mother does more than give birth; she shapes life.

The quotations herein remind us that a mother, as she raises her child, places her mark upon eternity. And we children are eternally grateful.

Chapter 1
A Mother Is...

$\mathcal{M}$otherhood is the
greatest privilege of life.

—

May Roper Coker

A mother is many things: She is the giver of life and love, the maker of house and home. She is chief cook and bottle washer, baby-sitter of last resort, provider, educator, doctor, disciplinarian, spiritual guide, counselor, health inspector, clothing consultant, taxi driver, and, of course, friend.

On the pages that follow, we consider various aspects of motherhood. It's a tough job, but someone has to do it… thank goodness for willing mothers.

A mother is…the holiest thing alive.

—Samuel Taylor Coleridge

The woman who creates and sustains a home
is a creator second only to God.

—Helen Hunt Jackson

Mother is the name for God on the lips and
in the hearts of little children.

—William Makepeace Thackeray

Mothers are the most important actors
in the grand drama of human progress.

—Elizabeth Cady Stanton

We bear the world, and we make it.
There was never a great man
who had not a great mother.

—*Olive Schreiner*

It's the mother who can cure her child's tears.

—*African Proverb*

Every mother is like Moses. She does not enter
the promised land. She prepares a world
she will not see.

—*Pope Paul VI*

The mother is the unchartered servant of the future.

—*Katherine Anthony*

Her children arise up, and call her blessed.

—Proverbs 31:28

Children are the anchors that hold a mother to life.

—Sophocles

The God to whom little boys say their prayers
has a face very much like their mother's.

—Sir James M. Barrie

A mother understands what her child *doesn't* say.

—Yiddish Proverb

Like mother, like daughter.

—*Old Saying*

What the mother sings to the cradle goes
all the way down to the coffin.

—*Henry Ward Beecher*

The role of mother is probably the most
important career a woman can have.

—*Janet Mary Riley*

A mother is not a person to lean on
but a person to make leaning unnecessary.

—*Dorothy Canfield Fisher*

As a mother, my job is to take care of the possible
and trust God with the impossible.

—*Ruth Bell Graham*

Most mothers are instinctive philosophers.

—*Harriet Beecher Stowe*

Motherhood is the biggest on-the-job training
program in existence today.

—*Erma Bombeck*

Motherhood is more art than science.

—*Melinda Marshall*

Who ran to help me when I fell,
        And would some pretty story tell,
        Or kiss the place to make it well?
        My mother.

—Ann Taylor

Our mother interposes herself between us and the world,
        protecting us from overwhelming anxiety.
        We shall have no greater need
        than this need for our mother.

—Judith Viorst

Be thou then, O thou dear Mother,
        my atmosphere; my happier world.

—Gerard Manley Hopkins

God could not be everywhere, so He made mothers.

—Jewish Proverb

The best academy is a mother's knee.

—James Russell Lowell

Every mother thinks her child is beautiful.

—Yiddish Proverb

Mother's Change The World...
One Child At a Time

Mothers shape the world as they shape the lives of their children. Abraham Lincoln spoke for grateful children everywhere when he observed, "All that I am, or all that I hope to be, I owe to my angel mother." In truth, we all owe to our mothers debts that we can never fully repay.

It has been said that the hand that rocks the cradle rules the world. Such is the power of motherhood. May we, as thankful sons and daughters, honor and praise those women who continue to change the world one child at a time.

A good woman is
the best thing on earth.
We can never estimate
the debt we owe to
godly wives and mothers.

—

Vance Havner

Chapter 2
Family

$\mathcal{A}$ family is one of
nature's masterpieces.

—

George Santayana

*T*o belong to a happy family is among the richest blessings known to man. But this blessing is not gifted from above with no strings attached. Happiness within the family must be earned by loving parents and their responsible children.

An old proverb reminds us, "When the family is together, the soul is at peace." The mother, as centerpiece of the household, helps hold the family together. But she, by herself, cannot create family harmony. Family living is a team sport that requires cooperation from fathers, daughters, sons, and the rest of the clan.

Raising a family is more art than science, more guesswork than certainty. But one thing remains sure: When the family is together, mother is the officer of the peace. On the pages that follow, we consider an assortment of peace offerings.

What we learn within the family are
  the most unforgettable lessons that our lives
  will ever teach us.

—Maggie Scarf

The mother! She is what keeps the family intact.
  It is proved. A fact.

—Anna F. Trevisan

A happy family is but an earlier heaven.

—Sir John Bowring

Call it a clan, call it a network, call it a tribe,
  call it a family. Whatever you call it,
  whoever you are, you need one.

—Jane Howard

A family is the school of duties founded on love.

—Felix Adler

A large family gives beauty to a house.

—Indian Proverb

Family life! The United Nations is child's play
        compared to the tugs and splits and need
        to understand and forgive in any family.

—May Sarton

A family is a unit composed not only
        of children, but of men, women,
        an occasional animal, and the common cold.

—Ogden Nash

Nobody's family can hang out the sign
"Nothing the Matter Here."

—*Chinese Proverb*

All happy families resemble one another;
every unhappy family is unhappy
in its own way.

—*Leo Tolstoy*

A family is the we of me.

—*Carson McCullers*

A family divided against itself will perish together.

—*Indian Proverb*

Healthy families are our greatest national resource.

—*Dolores Curran*

As the family goes, so goes the nation and
so goes the whole world in which we live.

—*Pope John Paul II*

You leave home to seek your fortune, and when
you get it, you go home and share it with your family.

—*Anita Baker*

Heirlooms we don't have in our family.
But stories we've got.

—*Rose Chernin*

Bringing up a family should be an adventure
      not an anxious discipline in which everybody
         is constantly graded for performance.

—Milton R. Sapirstein

Spoil your husband, but don't spoil your children.
         That's my philosophy.

—Louise Sevier Giddings Currey

What families have in common the world around
      is that they are the place where people learn
         who they are and how to be that way.

—Jean Illsley Clarke

Money can build or buy a house. Add love to that
and you have a home. Add God to that
and you have a temple.

—*Anne Ortland*

Comparison is a death knell to sibling harmony.

—*Elizabeth Fishel*

Honor your father-in-law and mother-in-law,
for they are now your parents.

—*Yiddish Saying*

I think we're seeing in working mothers a change
from "Thank God it's Friday"
to "Thank God it's Monday."

—*Ann Diehl*

*G*overn a family as
you would cook a small fish:
very gently.

—

Chinese Proverb

The Cornerstone of the Family

Who understands the importance of family more than mothers? After all, a family is a mother's creation (accomplished, of course, with the obvious participation of father).

Mothers shape the world one family at a time. Family life is the foundation of human existence and mother is the cornerstone upon which the family is built.

*H*e knew without a doubt
that in wife and child he had
the only treasures that really
mattered anyway.

—

Lewis Grizzard

Chapter 3
Love

*L*ove stretches your heart
and makes you big inside.

—

Margaret Walker

*G*ood mothers come in a wide range of shapes, sizes, colors, temperaments and nationalities, but they all share a singular trait: maternal love. Sometimes, that devotion is tested to the limits. From time to time, even well-intended children behave in ways that only a mother could love.

The common denominator of every magnificent mom is a heart big enough to love all of us kids—in spite of ourselves.

Love yourself first.

—*Lucille Ball*

Being a mother, as far as I can tell, is a constantly
evolving process of adapting to the needs
of your child while also changing and
growing as a person in your own right.

—*Deborah Insel*

Love is patient; love is kind and envies no one.
Love is never boastful, nor conceited, nor rude;
never selfish, not quick to take offense.

—*I Corinthians 13:4-5*

Love is a great beautifier.

—*Louisa May Alcott*

Love is the subtlest force in the world.

—*Mohandas Gandhi*

A successful marriage requires falling in love
many times, always with the same person.

—*Mignon McLaughlin*

Love is, above all, the gift of oneself.

—*Jean Anouilh*

The giving of love is an education in itself.

—Eleanor Roosevelt

A successful marriage is not a gift, it is an achievement.

—Ann Landers

There is nothing more lovely in life than the union
of two people whose love for one another has grown
through the years from the small acorn of passion
to a great-rooted tree.

—Vita Sackville-West

A good marriage is one which allows
for change and growth in the individuals
and in the way they express their love.

—Pearl Buck

Love does not consist in gazing at each other but
in looking outward together in the same direction.

—*Antoine de Saint Exupéry*

Nothing in life is as good as the marriage of
true minds between man and woman. As good?
It is life itself.

—*Pearl Buck*

Be completely humble and gentle; be patient
bearing with one another in love.

—*Ephesians 4:2*

And now abideth faith, hope, love, these three;
but the greatest of these is love.

—*I Corinthians 13:13*

Maternal love: a miraculous substance
which God multiplies as he divides it.

—Victor Hugo

Yet have I looked into my mother's eyes and seen
the light that never was on sea or land,
the light of love, pure love and true,
and on that love I bet my life.

—G. A. Studdert Kennedy

If you love only those who love you,
what reward can you expect?

—Matthew 5:46

Love is an act of will, namely, both intention
and an action.

—M. Scott Peck

Life is the flower of which love is the honey.

—*Victor Hugo*

A palace without affection is a poor hovel, and
the leanest hut with love in it is a palace for the soul.

—*Robert G. Ingersoll*

Parenthood is just the world's most intensive
course in love.

—*Polly Berrien Berends*

Everything in life that we really accept
undergoes a change; so suffering must
become love. That is the mystery.

—*Katherine Mansfield*

The fragrance always remains in the hand
                    that gives the rose.

—*Heda Bejar*

Youth fades; love droops; the leaves of friendship fall.
    A mother's secret love outlives them all.

—*Oliver Wendell Holmes, Sr.*

Love dies only when growth stops.

—*Leo Buscaglia*

It's not love's going that hurts my days,
        But that it went in little ways.

—*Edna St. Vincent Millay*

Life minus love equals zero.

—*George Sweeting*

If one wishes to know love, one must live love.

—*Leo Buscaglia*

When the evening of this life comes,
　　　　we shall be judged on love.

—*St. John of the Cross*

Whoever loves true love will love true life.

—*Elizabeth Barrett Browning*

$\mathcal{A}$ mother's love!
O holy, boundless thing!
Fountain whose waters
never cease to spring.

—

Marguerite Blessington

Lessons of Love

The first lesson a caring mother teaches her child is the lesson of love. A mother's love is like no other, a gift that is freely given, demonstrated by deed and word. Mothers give life and sustain it. If sacrifices must be made for the good of their children, loving mothers make those sacrifices without hesitation. And, every time a mother gives of herself, every time she hugs her baby or wipes away a tear, the child learns another lesson...in love.

*L*ove is the key
to every good.

—

Doris Lessing

Chapter 4
The Home

*M*ake yourself happy
where you are adored.

—

Isabella de' Medici Orsini

*T*he noted jurist Oliver Wendell Holmes, Jr. once observed, "Anywhere we love is home." All who have experienced the warmth of a love-filled household can second that emotion.

Home is not simply a place; it is a state of mind, built as much with love as with brick and mortar. The size of a house is relatively unimportant; the collective size of the hearts that dwell inside is all-important.

On the pages that follow, notable men and women share their blueprints for the greatest structure known to mankind: a happy home.

Home is the place where the great are small
and the small are great.

—*Robert Savage*

Make two homes for thyself: one actual home
and another spiritual home which thou
art to carry with thee always.

—*St. Catherine of Siena*

Home is any four walls that enclose the right person.

—*Helen Rowland*

Lonely? Dull? Not as long as I can have
        our friends gather around our fireplace
        or about our stone table for a picnic
        under the maples in the summer.

—Nancy Ford Cones

A house may draw visitors, but it is the
        possessor alone that can detain them.

—Charles Caleb Colton

The ornament of a house is the friends who frequent it.

—Ralph Waldo Emerson

We need not power or splendor;
Wide hall or lordly dome;
The good, the true, the tender,
These form the wealth of home.

—*Sarah Josepha Hale*

The ideal of happiness has always taken material form
in the house, whether cottage or castle. It stands for
permanence and separation from the world.

—*Simone de Beauvoir*

Radio, sewing machine, book ends, ironing board
and that great piano lamp—peace,
that's what I like.

—*Eudora Welty*

Our only chance for survival lies in creating
our own little islands of sanity and order,
in making little havens of our homes.

—*Sue Kaufman*

A house is no home unless it contains food
and fire for the mind as well as for the body.

—*Margaret Fuller*

Home is not where you live
but where they understand you.

—*Christian Morgenstern*

Home is a restaurant which never closes.

—*Anonymous*

God forbid that I should will any to do that
in my house which
I would not willingly do myself.

—*Margaret Clitherow*

Whatever the times, one thing will never change:
Fathers and mothers, if you have children,
they must come first. Your success as a family,
our success as a society, depends not on what
happens in the White House, but what happens
inside your house.

—*Barbara Bush*

Housekeeping is no joke.

—*Louisa May Alcott*

Cleaning your house while your kids are still growing
is like shoveling the walk
before it stops snowing.

—*Phyllis Diller*

They that think much and are not willing to do
such base things as housework have little regard
of well-doing or knowledge of themselves.

—*St. Margaret Clitherow*

Instant availability without continuous presence
is probably the best role a mother can play.

—*Lotte Bailyn*

Home—that blessed word which opens
to the human heart the most perfect
glimpse of Heaven.

—*Lydia M. Child*

It is a proud moment in a woman's life to reign
supreme within four walls; to be the one
to whom all questions of domestic pleasure
and economy are referred.

—*Elizabeth Cady Stanton*

To the old saying that "man built the house, but woman made it a home" might be added the modern supplement that woman accepted cooking as a chore but man has made of it a recreation.

—*Emily Post*

It is certainly true that housekeeping cares bring with them a thousand endearing compensations.

—*Marceline Desbordes-Valmore*

Creating a warm, caring, supportive, encouraging environment is probably the most important thing you can do for your family.

—*Stephen Covey*

A home is the place of last resort, open all night.

—*Ambrose Bierce*

There is nothing like staying at home for real comfort.

—*Jane Austen*

It takes a heap of lovin' in a house to make it a home.

—*Edgar A. Guest*

A good laugh is sunshine in a house.

—*William Makepeace Thackeray*

Charity too often not only begins but ends at home.

—*Anonymous*

The way you treat any relationship in the family
will eventually affect every relationship
in the family.

—*Stephen Covey*

Home is where the mortgage is.

—*Anonymous*

Better a hundred enemies
outside the house
than one inside.

—

Arabian Proverb

A Mother's Optimism

A mother's attitude is contagious. If she is optimistic and upbeat, her family tends to be optimistic and upbeat. But, if a mother falls prey to pessimism and doubt, her family suffers right along with her.

Wise moms understand the power of positive thinking, and they understand that positive thoughts are contagious. Savvy mothers share a message of encouragement and hope with those around them, starting with members of their family. When they do, their children learn this ironclad formula for living: as we think, so shall we become.

Home wasn't built
in a day.

—

Jane Ace

Chapter 5
Children

$\mathcal{A}$ child is the greatest poem
ever known.

—

Christopher Morley

*W*ere it not for kids, motherhood would be a breeze. But, children, of course, are the singular requirement of a mother's job description. Raising a family requires an endless supply of love, patience, understanding, and work. But, every mother knows that the potential payoff is worth the effort.

Henry Ward Beecher proclaimed, "Children are the hands by which we take hold of heaven." A mother, by taking firm hold of her child's hand, creates a little piece of heaven on earth. The following quotations celebrate the joy of creation.

Of all the haunting moments of motherhood,
few rank with hearing your own words
come out of your daughter's mouth.

—*Victoria Secunda*

Before I got married, I had six theories about
bringing up children; now I have six children
and no theories.

—*Lord Rochester*

People who say they sleep like a baby
usually don't have one.

—*Leo Burke*

A baby is God's opinion that life should go on.

—*Carl Sandburg*

A child is a beam of sunlight
from the Infinite and Eternal.

—*Lyman Abbott*

Kids are great. They are exciting. Their potential
is simply phenomenal. And in any given family there
is the potential to change the world....

—*Maxine Hancock*

A child is someone who stands
halfway between an adult and a TV set.

—*Anonymous*

All children are artists, and it is an indictment
   of our culture that so many of them lose their creativity,
         their unfettered imaginations,
            as they grow older.

—Madeleine L'Engle

Every child born into the world is a new thought of
      God, an ever-fresh and radiant possibility.

—Kate Douglas Wiggin

Insanity is hereditary: you can get it from your children.

—Sam Levenson

No one has yet fully realized the wealth
of sympathy, kindness and generosity hidden
in the soul of a child.

—Emma Goldman

Wherever children are learning,
there dwells the Divine Presence.

—Old Saying

Children miss nothing in sizing up their parents.
If you are only half-convinced of your beliefs,
they will quickly discern that fact.

—James Dobson

Even when freshly washed and relieved of all
  obvious confections, children tend to be sticky.

—Fran Lebowitz

For the parents of a Little Leaguer, a baseball game
  is simply a nervous breakdown into innings.

—Earl Wilson

Adorable children are considered to be the
  general property of the human race.
  Rude children belong to their mothers.

—Judith Martin

Sometimes when I look at all my children,
I say to myself,
"Lillian, you should have stayed a virgin."
—*Lillian Carter*

I looked on raising children not only as a work
of love and duty but as a profession that
demanded the best that I could bring to it.
—*Rose Kennedy*

Children are likely to live up to
what you believe of them.
—*Lady Bird Johnson*

Parents of young children should realize that
      few people will find their children
        as enchanting as they do.

                                   —Barbara Walters

All children alarm their parents,
      if only because you are forever expecting
        to encounter yourself.

                                     —Gore Vidal

What we desire our children to become,
      we must endeavor to be before them.

                                   —Andrew Combe

Discipline does not break a child's spirit half
as often as the lack of it breaks a parent's heart.

—Anonymous

When a child enters the world through you,
it alters everything.

—Jane Fonda

The mother's heart is the child's schoolroom.

—Henry Ward Beecher

Never allow your child to call you by your
first name. He hasn't known you long enough.

—Fran Lebowitz

No matter how old a mother is,
she watches her middle-aged children
for signs of improvement.

—Florida Scott-Maxwell

Ask your child what he wants for dinner
only if he's buying.

—Fran Lebowitz

What feeling is so nice as a child's hand in yours?
So small, so soft and warm, like a kitten huddling
in the shelter of your clasp.

—*Marjorie Holmes*

What good mothers and fathers instinctively
feel like doing for their babies
is usually best after all.

—*Benjamin Spock*

The character and history of each child may
be a new and poetic experience to the parent,
if he will let it.

—*Margaret Fuller*

Parents learn a lot from their children
about coping with life.

—Muriel Spark

Love your children with all your hearts,
love them enough to discipline them
before it is too late.

—Lavina Christensen Fugal

At every step the child should be allowed to meet
the real experiences of life; the thorns should never
be plucked from their roses.

—Ellen Key

Loving a child doesn't mean giving in to all his whims;
to love him is to bring out the best in him,
to teach him to love what is difficult.

—*Nadia Boulanger*

The goal of disciplining our children is to
encourage their growth as respectful, responsible,
self-disciplined individuals.

—*Don H. Highlander*

Children have more need of models than of critics.

—*Joseph Joubert*

The debt of gratitude we owe our mother
and father goes forward, not backward.
What we owe our parents is the bill
presented to us by our children.

—*Nancy Friday*

Children are God's small interpreters.

—*John Greenleaf Whittier*

Our children are not going to be just *our* children—
they are going to be other people's husbands
and wives and the parents
of our grandchildren.

—*Mary S. Calderone*

Let every father and mother understand
      that when their child is three years old,
      they have done more than half of all
      they will ever do for its character.

—Horace Bushnell

We are together, my child and I, mother and child,
      yes, but *sisters* really, against whatever denies
      us all that we are.

—Alice Walker

Every child born into the world is a new thought
      of God, an ever-fresh and radiant possibility.

—Kate Douglas Wiggin

If you want a baby, have a new one.
Don't baby the old one.

—*Jessamyn West*

One hour with a child is like a ten-mile run.

—*Joan Benoit Samuelson*

Celebrate your children's achievements.

—*Anonymous*

The voice of parents is the voice of gods,
for to their children, they are heaven's lieutenants.

—*William Shakespeare*

The best things you can give children,
next to good habits, are good memories.

—*Sydney J. Harris*

Parents must get across the idea that "I love you always,
but sometimes I do not love your behavior."

—*Amy Vanderbilt*

It takes courage to let our children go, but we are
trustees and stewards and have to hand them
back to life—to God.
We have to love them and lose them.

—*Alfred Torrie*

A child's tears move
the heavens themselves.

—

Old Saying

A Mother's Encouragement

A mother's encouragement is a priceless gift to a child. And how can we be most encouraging to our children? The answer is found, in part, by reminding ourselves what genuine encouragement is and what it is not.

The dictionary defines encouragement as "the act of inspiring courage and confidence." Genuine encouragement is not idle flattery. It is, instead, the transfer of courage from one person to another (in this case, from mother to child). Genuine encouragement is a firm reminder to the child of his or her talents, strengths, resources, and opportunities. Encouragement is confidence shared...and multiplied.

Every child comes with
the message that God is not
yet discouraged of man.

—

Tagore

Chapter 6
Happiness

$\mathcal{A}$ll times are beautiful
for those who maintain
joy within themselves.

—

Rosalia Castro

*H*er child's happiness is a mother's ambition. But, as time passes and adulthood approaches, happiness becomes the responsibility of the child, not the parent. No one, not even a loving mother, can bestow the gift of contentment; each of us must earn it for ourselves.

While unable to bestow peace of mind, a thoughtful mother *can* show her child that peace of mind is possible. She does so by example not decree.

On the pages that follow, notable men and women share practical prescriptions for happiness. Every mother can teach these lessons *and* live by them…and should.

Take time each day to do something silly.

—*Philipa Walker*

Always laugh when you can; it is cheap medicine.
Merriment is a philosophy not well understood.
It is the sunny side of existence.

—*George Gordon Byron*

Until you make peace with who you are,
you'll never be content with what you have.

—*Doris Mortman*

Happiness is not a goal; it is a by-product.

—*Eleanor Roosevelt*

Happiness is a by-product of an effort
    to make someone else happy.

—*Gretta Palmer*

Happy people plan actions, they don't plan results.

—*Dennis Wholey*

Growth itself contains the germ of happiness.

—*Pearl Buck*

Happiness walks on busy feet.

—*Kitte Turmell*

If only we'd stop trying to be happy,
             we'd have a pretty good time.

—*Edith Wharton*

A mediocre idea that generates enthusiasm
             will go farther than a great idea
             that inspires no one.

—*Mary Kay Ashe*

Change is an easy panacea. It takes character
to stay in one place and be happy there.
—*Elizabeth Clarke Dunn*

It isn't the great big pleasures that count
the most; it's making a great deal out
of the little ones.
—*Jean Webster*

I have the greatest of all riches:
that of not desiring them.
—*Eleonora Duse*

Be content with such things as ye have.
—*Hebrews 13:5*

One must never look for happiness.
One meets it by the way.

—*Isabelle Eberhardt*

It is not easy to find happiness in ourselves,
and it is not possible to find it elsewhere.

—*Agnes Repplier*

True happiness is not attained through
self-gratification but through fidelity
to a worthy cause.

—*Helen Keller*

Laughter is like premium gasoline:
> It helps take the knock out of living.

> *—Anonymous*

Talk happiness. The world is sad enough
> without your woe.

> *—Ella Wheeler Wilcox*

Happiness is not a matter of events;
> it depends upon the tides of the minds.

> *—Alice Meynell*

Happiness is a life spent learning, earning and yearning.

—Lillian Gish

I had a pleasant time with my mind, for it was happy.

—Louisa May Alcott

Be happy. It's one way of being wise.

—Colette

No one's happiness but my own
> is in my power to achieve or to destroy.

—*Ayn Rand*

New happiness too must be learned to bear.

—*Marie von Ebner-Eschenbach*

Birds sing after a storm; why shouldn't people
> feel as free to delight in
> whatever remains to them?

—*Rose Kennedy*

*L*aughter is the music
of the world.

—

Anonymous

And Let Me Laugh

Lord, when I begin to take myself or my life too seriously, let me laugh.

When I rush from place to place, slow me down, Lord. Give me Your perspective, Your wisdom, and Your peace. And let me laugh.

When the day is cloudy, keep me mindful that above the clouds, the sun still shines. And let me laugh.

Each morning, when I open my eyes to a world of glorious possibilities, let me give thanks for the gift of life, and then, let me make the most of that gift. Let me strive toward a worthy purpose, and let me celebrate each day with a song, and a smile, and a prayer…and, let me laugh.

—*Criswell Freeman*

*L*aughter is the
shortest distance
between two people.

—

Victor Borge

Chapter 7
Faith

Without faith, nothing
is possible. With it,
nothing is impossible.

—

Mary McLeod Bethune

ife is a grand adventure made great by faith.
Enduring faith is first experienced on the mother's knee. There, the child learns to trust not only in the parent but also the world.

If *you're* looking for a message to share with future generations, preach the gospel of faith: faith in the future, faith in one's fellow man, and faith in the Hand that shapes eternity. No message is more important.

You're not free until you've been made captive
by supreme belief.

—*Marianne Moore*

To eat bread without hope is still slowly
to starve to death.

—*Pearl Buck*

Sad soul, take comfort nor forget,
The sunrise never failed us yet.

—*Celia Thaxter*

An optimistic mind is a healthy mind.

—*Loretta Young*

Faith is to believe in something not yet proved
and to underwrite it with our lives. It is the
only way we can leave the future open.

—*Lillian Smith*

Faith is the assertion of a possibility
against all probabilities.

—*Ethelbert Stauffer*

Faith is putting all your eggs in God's basket,
then counting your blessings before they hatch.

—*Ramona C. Carroll*

Faith is the key to fit the door of hope,
    but there is no power anywhere like love
        for turning it.

—*Elaine Emans*

Faith is the substance of things hoped for,
    the evidence of things not seen.

—*Hebrews: 11:1*

Faith is the subtle chain which binds us to the infinite.

—*Elizabeth Oakes Smith*

Faith sees the invisible, believes the incredible
and receives the impossible.

—Anonymous

Faith is the sturdiest of the virtues.
It is the virtue of the storm, just as happiness
is the virtue of sunshine.

—Ruth Benedict

I was always looking outside myself for strength
and confidence, but it comes from within.
It was there all the time.

—Anna Freud

Hope deferred maketh the heart sick.

—Proverbs 13:12

The primary cause of unhappiness
         in the world today is lack of faith.

—Carl Jung

Faith is the flip side of fear.

—Susan Taylor

Faith is the only known cure for fear.

—Lena K. Sadler

Faith is like a radar that sees through the fog —
the reality of things at a distance that the
human eye cannot see.

—Corrie ten Boom

To have faith where you cannot see; to be
willing to work on in the dark; to be conscious
of the fact that there are better things on the way;
this is success.

—Katherine Logan

One of the things I learned the hard way was that
it doesn't pay to get discouraged. Keeping busy
and making optimism a way of life can restore
your faith in yourself.

—Lucille Ball

Build in darkness if you have faith.
　　　　When the light returns, you have made
　　　　of yourself a fortress which is impregnable.

—Olga Rosmanith

So with faith, if it does not lead to action,
　　　　it is in itself a lifeless thing.

—James 2:17

It is by believing in roses that one brings them to bloom.

—French Proverb

Faith During Difficult Times

Corrie ten Boom observed, "Faith is an activity. It is something that has to be applied." But, during times of adversity, the application of faith can be difficult indeed. Tough times have a way of convincing us that all is lost. Of course, all is most certainly *not* lost. What's needed is a heaping helping of hope mixed with a willingness to tackle the problem, whatever it may be.

If you are approaching a crossroads, approach it optimistically. If you are enduring tough times, never abandon hope in your future or yourself. And, if you are in need of a surefire remedy for the inevitable cuts and scrapes of life, try this prescription: take a double dose of faith and combine it with swift action targeted specifically at solving the problem. Chances are, you'll feel much better in the morning.

I pray hard, work hard,
and leave the rest to God.

—

Florence Griffith Joyner

Chapter 8
Life

How we spend our days is,
of course,
how we spend our lives.

—

Annie Dillard

*F*irst mothers give life, then they teach it. The best form of maternal instruction is, of course, example. A mother's actions speak more loudly than her words, but her words, too, are important. If a mother wishes to teach the important lessons of life, she must speak wisely and act wisely, but not necessarily in that order.

On the following pages, we consider a few lessons that any mother would be proud to teach *and* to live by.

When you were born, you cried and the world rejoiced!
Live your life in such a manner that when you die,
the world cries and you rejoice.

—*Old Indian Saying*

If you let yourself be absorbed completely,
if you surrender completely to the moments
as they pass, you live more richly.

—*Anne Morrow Lindbergh*

All of us tend to put off living. We are all dreaming
of some magical rose garden over the horizon
instead of enjoying the roses that are blooming
outside our windows today.

—*Dale Carnegie*

Life is either a daring adventure or nothing.
>>> To keep our faces toward change and behave
>>> like free spirits in the presence of fate
>>> is strength undefeatable.

—Helen Keller

No one grows old by living,
>>> only by losing interest in living.

—Marie Beynon Ray

It's only when we truly know and understand that
>>> we have a limited time on earth—and that we have
>>> no way of knowing when our time is up—that we
>>> will begin to live each day to the fullest,
>>> as if it were the only one we had.

—Elisabeth Kübler-Ross

To live fully, outwardly and inwardly, not to ignore
external reality for the sake of the inner life,
or the reverse—that's quite a task.

—*Etty Hillesum*

We're all in this together—by ourselves.

—*Lily Tomlin*

Don't hurry, don't worry. You're only here for
a short time. So be sure to stop and smell the roses.

—*Walter Hagen*

They are committing murder who merely live.

—*May Sarton*

I am one of those people who just can't help
getting a kick out of life—even when it's
a kick in the teeth.

—*Polly Adler*

To live in and for the moment is deadly serious work,
fun of the most exhausting sort.

—*Barbara Grizzuti Harrison*

Life begets life. Energy creates energy. It is
by spending oneself that one becomes rich.

—*Sarah Bernhardt*

She seems to have had the ability to stand
firmly on the rock of her past, while living
completely and unregretfully in the present.

—*Madeleine L'Engle*

I love my past. I love my present. I'm not ashamed
of what I've had, and I'm not sad because
I have it no longer.

—*Colette*

I have learned to live each day as it comes and
not to borrow trouble by dreading tomorrow.
It is the dark menace of the future
that makes cowards of us.

—*Dorothy Dix*

Yesterday is a cancelled check; tomorrow
is a promissory note; today is the only cash
you have—so spend it wisely.

—Kay Lyons

A man is not old until regrets take
the place of his dreams.

—John Barrymore

The past is finished. There is nothing to be gained
by going over it. Whatever it gave us in the experiences
it brought us was something we had to know.

—Rebecca Beard

Living is a form of not being sure. We guess.
We may be wrong, but we take leap
after leap in the dark.

—*Agnes de Mille*

Mistakes are part of the dues one pays for a full life.

—*Sophia Loren*

Remorse is the poison of life.

—*Charlotte Brontë*

Life is meant to be lived, and curiosity
must be kept alive. One must never,
for whatever reason, turn his back on life.

—*Eleanor Roosevelt*

Life is raw material. We are artisans.

—*Cathy Better*

Life is what we make it. Always has been.
Always will be.

—*Grandma Moses*

You don't get to choose how you're going to die,
or when. You can only decide
how you're going to live. Now!

—*Joan Baez*

Life has got to be lived—that's all there is to it.

—*Eleanor Roosevelt*

Learn to drink the cup of life as it comes.

—Agnes Turnbull

I don't want to get to the end of my life
    and find that I lived just the length of it.
    I want to have lived the width of it as well.

—Diane Ackerman

Celebrating Life

When we celebrate life, life has a way of celebrating us. But, if we allow fears and regrets to rule our thoughts, we experience predictably poor results. We must, therefore, resolve to live abundantly, thankfully, expectantly, and joyfully—and we must teach our children to do the same.

From this day forward, resolve to make your life a series of one-day celebrations. Give thanks for your blessings and enjoy every step of your journey, realizing that each day holds its own unique treasures but that those treasures are not yours until you claim them.

$\mathcal{G}$od, give me work till
my life shall end and
life till my work is done.

—

Winifred Holtby

Chapter 9
Memories
of Mom

$\mathcal{M}$ama gave us the role model
of someone who knew how
to juggle. She was always there,
and yet she was always working.
We thought she was the most
beautiful woman alive.

—

Cokie Roberts

$\mathcal{T}$he present moment is fleeting, and the future is uncertain. The past, however, is now permanently assigned to the history books. And, it becomes a priceless treasure for those who are wise enough to assemble a collection of happy memories.

Happy memories are precious, but happy memories of mom are among the most precious of all. In this chapter, notable men and women share recollections of memorable mothers. Enjoy!

Nothing is as precious as my mama's memory.

—*Dolly Parton*

My dad ended up selling vacuum cleaners,
and my mom got a job as a secretary.
They never got rich, and they never got famous,
but they showed me that you do things
for a purpose.

—*Julia Roberts*

We didn't know how poor we were.
We were rich as a family.

—*Florence Griffith Joyner*

Someday this girl will be the first lady of something.

—*Jackie Joyner-Kersee's grandmother*

The household was a full-time occupation.
I have one of the best mothers anyone could have.

—*Arnold Schwarzenegger*

My mother is as tough as nails; a great mother
and a great woman, very independent.
She's constantly challenging herself. She has told me
that much has been given to me,
and therefore I should do something with it.

—*Maria Shriver*

My parents encouraged me to read and think.

—Gwendolyn Brooks

I had a wonderful, happy childhood.
I think my parents liked to inspire creativity
and productivity in their children.
Our happiness was important to them.

—John Travolta

I think maybe comedy was part of my way of connecting
with my mother. I'd make Mommy laugh
and everything was OK.
That's where it started.

—Robin Williams

My parents wanted to make sure that if we
had a talent, we got the chance to develop it.

—Alison Krauss

My father was on the road a great deal, and
my mother ran the family. She believed in
discipline. There was none of that Hollywood
scene of the star's spoiled kids.

—Natalie Cole

My mother worked at home as a seamstress.
She would get angry if she was given a bad dress
to work on. Subliminally, that stuck. I don't want
to sing a song unless it's great.

—Tony Bennett

My mother was a great storyteller,
a very free spirit who believed in creativity
and freedom of expression.

—*Anne Rice*

My mother taught me how to be inquisitive.

—*Heloise*

My mother was also my best friend.
She left me with a rich endowment
of ideas and memories.

—*Faith Ringgold*

The big factor in my life, in terms of my career,
has always been my mother. She taught me that you
have to watch out for the opportunities and
not be afraid to take risks.

—*Lesley Stahl*

My signature appears on $60 billion of U.S. currency.
More importantly, however, is the signature that
appears on my life—the strong, proud,
assertive handwriting
of a loving mother and father.

—*Katherine D. Ortega,*
Treasurer of the United States

It used to get to me when Mama, who is my
biggest critic, was in the audience. But now that
I'm a mama myself, I realize
that she loves me regardless of how I do.

—*Reba McEntire*

She was always
my best girl.

—

Elvis Presley

The Power of Positive Memories

Over a lifetime, we all live through a wide range of experiences: some good, some not-so-good, and some tragic. When we allow ourselves to focus on the inevitable disappointments and hardships of the past, we create additional burdens for ourselves and for our families. A far better strategy is to build an extensive collection of happy memories and to re-visit those memories often.

Whenever life throws you a curveball, hit it and forget it. Don't stay mired in the pit of bitterness. Don't become a prisoner of hatred, envy, or regret. Instead, learn the lessons that must be learned from your experiences, and move on. When you do, you'll leave plenty of room for the kind of memories that will enrich your life, the kind of memories that are rightfully yours: the happy kind.

$\mathcal{M}$y mother was all mother.

—

Ella Fitzgerald

Chapter 10
Motherly Advice

If you always do
what interests you,
at least one person
will be pleased.

—

Mother's Advice to Katharine Hepburn

*F*ew things in life are more useful than mothers' advice. But the supply of this advice vastly outpaces its demand. Children seem destined to make their own mistakes despite parental preachments or maternal mandates. Each generation, it appears, must learn anew the lessons of the last.

The Talmud reminds us that "He who is best taught first learned from his mother." In this chapter, we consider tried-and-true motherly advice that is often taught and sometimes learned. All of us, mothers and children alike, can benefit from a refresher course.

She'd always say to me, "Don't think that your looks
are going to help in the long run, because you'll
be pretty today and someone else will be prettier
tomorrow. Make sure you improve your brain,
because that will make you interesting."

—*Maria Shriver*

She taught me to see beauty in all things around me;
that inside each thing a spirit lived, that it was vital,
too, regardless of whether it was only a leaf or
a blade of grass, and by recognizing its life and beauty,
I was accepting God.

—*Maria Campbell*

My mother said to me, "If you become
    a soldier, you'll be a general; if you become
    a monk, you'll end up as the pope." Instead,
    I became a painter and wound up as Picasso.

—Pablo Picasso

Fill what's empty. Empty what's full.
    And scratch where it itches.

—Alice Roosevelt Longworth

Children find comfort in flaws, ignorance
    and insecurities similar to their own.
    I love my mother for letting me see hers.

—Erma Bombeck

In youth we learn. In age we understand.

—Marie von Ebner-Eschenbach

Keep the other person's well-being in mind
        when you feel an attack of soul-purging
            truth coming on.

—Betty White

People who fight fire with fire end up with ashes.

—Abigail Van Buren

Kind words can be short and easy to speak
 but their echoes are truly endless.

—Mother Teresa

If you judge people, you have no time to love them.

—Mother Teresa

It is by forgiving that one is forgiven.

—Mother Teresa

Nothing in life is to be feared.
It is only to be understood.

—

Marie Curie

The Joys and Frustrations of Motherhood

Motherhood is vastly rewarding, but, at times, frustrating. No family is perfect, and even the most understanding mom's patience can wear thin on occasion.

When you are tempted to lose your temper over the minor inconveniences of family life, don't. Count to ten, and, if that doesn't work, keep counting. If you find yourself mired in the pit of negativity, take time for a much-needed pit stop. As you slow down to gather your emotions, turn your thoughts to the blessings and the love that *have come* and *will come* from the family that calls you "Mom." And how many blessings should you count? Count to ten, and, if that doesn't work, keep counting.

Expect trouble as an inevitable part of life and repeat to yourself the most comforting words of all: This, too, shall pass.

—

Ann Landers

Chapter 11
Observations

$\mathcal{A}$ mother's patience is like
a tube of toothpaste:
It's never quite gone.

—

Anonymous

ow, we will conclude with a potpourri of observations about children, music, toothpaste, and other assorted topics near and dear to a mother's heart.

In Mom we trust...forever.

As a mother I have served longer than I expected.

—*Carol Emshwiller*

Five out of my five kids are too good
        to be true, thanks to their mother.
      She is a world-class mother.

—*Ross Perot*

I wanted to make music my mother would listen to.

—*Will Smith*

No man is poor who has a Godly mother.

—*Abraham Lincoln*

The warmest bed of all is Mother's.

—*Old Saying*

I guess what I've really discovered is the humanizing
effect of children in my life, stretching me,
humbling me. Maybe my thighs aren't as thin
as they used to be, maybe my getaways aren't
as glamorous. Still I like the woman that
motherhood has helped me to become.

—*Susan Lapinski*

There are no shortcuts to any place worth going.

—Beverly Sills

To know how to do something well is to enjoy it.

—Pearl Buck

What we are is God's gift to us.
What we become is our gift to God.

—Eleanor Powell

Most things have an escape clause,
             but children are forever.

                      —*Lewis Grizzard*

Service is the rent that you pay for room on this earth.

                      —*Shirley Chisholm*

Life is a flame that is always burning itself out,
             but it catches fire again every time
                a child is born.

                    —*George Bernard Shaw*